# POLICE OFFICER

BY CHRIS BOWMAN

BELLWETHER MEDIA · MINNEAPOLIS, MN

Are you ready to take it to the extreme?
Torque books thrust you into the action-packed world
of sports, vehicles, mystery, and adventure. These books
may include dirt, smoke, fire, and dangerous stunts.
**WARNING**: read at your own risk.

Library of Congress Cataloging-in-Publication Data

Bowman, Chris, 1990- author.
  Police Officer / by Chris Bowman.
     pages cm. -- (Torque: Dangerous Jobs)
  Summary: "Engaging images accompany information about police officers. The combination of
high-interest subject matter and light text is intended for students in grades 3 through 7"-- Provided
by publisher.
  Audience: Ages 7-12.
  Audience: Grades 3 to 7.
  Includes bibliographical references and index.
  ISBN 978-1-62617-112-1 (hardcover : alk. paper)
  1. Police--Juvenile literature.  I. Title.
  HV7922.B687 2014
  363.2023--dc23
                                    2013050256

This edition first published in 2015 by Bellwether Media, Inc.

Printed in the United States of America, North Mankato, MN.

# TABLE OF CONTENTS

# CHAPTER 1
# CAR CHASE!

A police officer is out patrolling the streets. Suddenly, a call comes in on his car radio. Another cop needs backup in a high-speed chase! The officer turns the car around and flips his lights on. He speeds after the car.

The **suspect** stops the car and starts running. The officer gets out and runs after him. He quickly catches up to the suspect. He tackles the man and handcuffs his wrists. Got him! The streets are safer thanks to the officer's actions.

# CHAPTER 2

# POLICE OFFICERS

Police officers serve and protect their communities. They make sure people follow city, state, and national laws. This includes **investigating** crimes, issuing tickets, and making arrests. Officers help people in need at accidents or other emergencies. They also teach their communities about being responsible citizens.

# United States Police Ranks

Chief of Police / Police Commissioner

Deputy Chief of Police / Deputy Commissioner

Commander

Captain

Lieutenant

Sergeant

Detective

Officer

A police officer's goal is to keep the peace. This means carrying out laws to keep people safe. Officers patrol public places on foot, bicycle, motorcycle, or car. They answer calls about complaints, **disturbances**, and accidents. At the scene, they arrest people who are a danger to others. Officers also make sure **victims** are okay. If needed, they give **first aid**.

Police officers are experts on **public safety**. Many officers study **criminal justice** in college. Before joining the force, officers pass a physical fitness test. They also must pass a personality test. Then they complete police academy training. Here, they learn how to patrol and safely use their **firearm**. They also learn how to keep suspects under control and search a crime scene for **evidence**.

# Physically Fit

Though fitness tests vary between forces, most U.S. police officers are tested on their ability to do the following:

- Do push-ups for one minute
- Do sit-ups for one minute
- Sprint for 328 yards (300 meters)
- Run for 1.5 miles (2.4 kilometers)

Officers wear belts with many gadgets to help them do their job. They carry a big flashlight and a pair of handcuffs. A radio connects them to other officers. For protection, officers carry **pepper spray** and a **baton**. They also carry an **electronic control device**, commonly called a Taser. Though they hope to never use it, officers carry a firearm and extra bullets.

electronic control device

handcuffs

## No Shot

Cops also commonly wear bulletproof vests. These protect the officers' bodies from guns and knives. Most of these vests are made of soft material. In really dangerous situations, officers wear hard bulletproof armor.

# CHAPTER 3
# DANGER!

Police officers never know what calls they will get while on duty. They have to be ready for anything. Most calls have little danger. However, officers put themselves at risk every time they stop someone. **Criminals** may become **violent**.

Other times, officers hurt themselves when helping others. Difficult tasks, such as rescuing accident victims, can be dangerous. Car accidents are another big risk for officers. Many cops spend a lot of time behind the wheel. They are more likely to be in high-speed car chases and traffic accidents.

## Unexpected Risks

Some of the dangers to officers are unseen. It can be hard for them to watch others experience violence and suffering. Officers sometimes need help dealing with the painful things they see on the job.

Police officers understand the risks of their job. They wear the badge anyway. Officers accept the challenges because they want to help people and keep everyone safe. They are ready to do what it takes to protect and serve.

## Tragedy on the Job

On January 15, 2013, Officer Kevin Tonn was killed on a burglary call in California. When Officer Tonn arrived at the scene, he approached a suspect for questioning. The suspect pulled out a gun and fired a deadly shot.

# Glossary

**baton**—a short stick carried by a police officer for self-defense

**criminal justice**—government practices that deal with crime and criminals

**criminals**—people who have committed crimes

**disturbances**—events that threaten the peace, health, or safety of an area; disturbances can include too much noise, fights, and riots.

**electronic control device**—a weapon that uses electricity to stun someone; police officers use electronic control devices in self-defense.

**evidence**—physical proof that supports a conclusion or explanation

**firearm**—a gun

**first aid**—emergency medical care given to a sick or injured person before he or she reaches a hospital

**investigating**—searching for clues to find out the facts about something

**pepper spray**—a spray that irritates the eyes and throat; police officers use pepper spray in self-defense.

**public safety**—the protection of the general public

**suspect**—a person who is believed to have committed a crime

**victims**—people who are hurt, killed, or made to suffer

**violent**—ready to use harmful physical force

# To Learn More

## AT THE LIBRARY

Bowman, Chris. *Animal Control Officer*. Minneapolis, Minn.: Bellwether Media, 2014.

Landau, Elaine. *Deadly High-Risk Jobs*. Minneapolis, Minn.: Lerner Publications Company, 2013.

Tisdale, Rachel. *Police Officers*. New York, N.Y.: Crabtree Pub. Co., 2012.

## ON THE WEB

Learning more about police officers is as easy as 1, 2, 3.

1. Go to www.factsurfer.com.

2. Enter "police officers" into the search box.

3. Click the "Surf" button and you will see a list of related web sites.

With factsurfer.com, finding more information is just a click away.

# Index